Chorley
in old picture postcards

by Jack Smith

European Library ZALTBOMMEL / THE NETHERLANDS

Acknowledgements

The author wishes to thank the following organisations and individuals for the use of photographs from their collections:

Chorley Central Library, The Chorley Guardian Newspaper, The Chorley and District Historical and Archaeological Society, Bolton Museum and Art Gallery.

The late J. Shaw. Also Mr. R. Severs and Mr. G. Bellis.

Although every attempt has been made to establish ownership of all photographs used in this publication, it has not been possible in every case. Should ownership be discoverd subsequently, corrections will be made to any further issues of this publication.

GB ISBN 90 288 1130 3

© 1998 European Library – Zaltbommel/The Netherlands

Introduction

The township is thought to have originated during Saxon Times, when the first settlement may have been established, some 1,000 years ago, give or take a couple of hundred years either way.

But the first known people to live close to where the town would later be established, and whose buried remains have been found, were living here about 3,000 years ago, during the Middle to Late Bronze Age.

The name of the town is believed to come from the stream which flows east to west, given the name 'Ceorle' or similar. The later part of the name 'ley' meaning a field or meadow. Thus Chorley was settled, on 'the field by the River Ceorle or Chor'.

On a steep hillside overlooking this river, the first 'chapel' was built, later to become established as the first church in the town in the 14th century, the population at this time being about 1,000 persons. This later became the Parish Church of St. Lawrence, the oldest church in the town today.

The town is situated on the edge of the Pennine Hills lying to the east, whilst westwards from Chorley, the Lancashire Plain stretches to the Irish Sea Coast, at its closest, about twenty miles away, at Southport. Apart from the 'Chorley' family, another of the town's famous families were the Standish'es, a branch of this family living at the Manor of Duxbury from the 14th century, circa 1335. This branch were the ancestors of Myles Standish, who sailed across to the New World with the Pilgrim Fathers.

During the Civil War period several local families were involved with the conflict, supporting one side or the other. Chorley was often described as 'a nest of recusants'.

The first Roman Catholic Church established in the town was in the year 1774, this was the church of St. Gregory, built in the Weld Bank area of the town. Previously, the Roman Catholics in the area had carried out their act of worship at the private chapel of the Chadwich Family at Burgh Hall, a short distance away from the site of the new church.

Over the centuries several historian/travellers have visited the town,. the first of these being Leland about 1550. He described the township as 'wonderfull, poor, with no market'. During the 17th century, Richard Blome visited Chorley. He said about it, that 'the town of Chorley was situated near the spring head of the river Chor. It is a small town, but its market is well stocked with yarn and provisions'. Another visitor to the town was the writer Defoe, but what he says about the town does not seem to have been recorded.

The economy of the town has been one of agriculture since the earliest times, its market for general goods and cattle has continued down to the present day, although cattle ceased being sold at the market in the late 1940s only. There are two markets in the town, one being a semi-covered one, the other is held in a large open area still called the 'cattle market', also nicknamed the 'Flat Iron'.

Industry came to the town during the 15th century, when the first powered industries were established, using the plentiful supply of water from the many streams near the town. The first of these powered mills was set up by Richard Arkwright in 1777.

In 1801, the population of Chorley was 4,516 persons. By 1831 it was up to 9,282. This was a time when the town was growing rapidly, much of the land being enclosed, and earmarked for development. The growth of the town was enhanced more so by the setting up of bleaching and cotton mills in the town, plus the coming of the railway and canal, together with coal mining and quarrying. The town had its first newspaper in 1864.

By 1881, the population had risen to 19,478, and some thirty or so cotton mills were at work in the town. Ten of these were spinning mills, the others were for weaving. Additionally, there were foundries, engineering works, a brewery, wagon and carriagemakers, and all the other ancillary businesses, which supplied the needs of the town; a town which now had sixteen smaller parishes under its administration. 1881 saw Chorley achieve the status of Municipal Borough, the town being described at the time as having 'streets well laid out to the advantage of vehicles and pedestrians, and having many churches and chapels, together with a library and hospital'.

During the 1880's, the telephone arrived in Chorley, the early numbers being taken by cotton mills, collieries, and bleachworks, followed by other shops and businesses in the town. All of which seem to have superseded the Town Hall only getting its own telephone number at the end of the decade.

The town's 'roots', in agriculture, were still being reflected in the Fairs, which were still being held into the 1890's. In March, horses, cattle and pigs were sold. In May it was horses only. In August and October, the fairs sold horses and cattle. In addition to the fairs held for the sale of cattle etc. two others, for the sale of general goods, were held in April and September. All of the above were in addition to the twice-weekly market which had been held from 1498.

By the end of the 19th century, the town, with its associated industrial growth, saw great expansion into the surrounding countryside. The increase in population led to the need for more shops, churches and recreational areas, for open spaces within the town had been built over. Recreation Grounds were created during the early years of the 1900's, one of these being used in 1913, when King George V and Queen Mary visited the town.

Theatres and cinemas had become established at this time, being well-patronised by the townsfolk of Chorley. One of the more popular ones was a wooden theatre run by one Mr. Testo Sante. This burned down in 1914, and was a great loss to the town at that time.

The coming of the motor vehicle to the town led to bus sevices being set up, firstly by the Lancashire and Yorkshire Railway Company, whose rail lines ran through the town. The bus companies also ran trips to local places of interest and to the seaside. These buses were called charabancs, their popularity being unrivalled in the 1920's.

In 1922, a War Memorial was given to the town in the form of a complete park. This was called Astley Park, having been privately owned since its building in 1578. Within the park, which is located near the middle of the town, is the old hall. This is open to the public and is famous for its decorated plasterwork ceilings. Within the park a War Memorial Cenotaph was built.

The manufacture of cottons, from spinning, weaving, dying and bleaching became the mainstay industry of the town through the 1920's and 30's, with foundries, coal mining, and other lesser industries. In 1931, the population of the town was 30,951; a town which was still growing, in physical size and prosperity.

Jack Smith

1   This view from about 1900 shows the approach to the town centre of Chorley from the north. This road, named Park Road, runs through the middle of the town, and is still, today, a through route, although the road's status as a 'trunk road' has been superseded. Park Road is so named due to its running alongside a park, named Astley Park. The entrance to this park can be seen on the right-hand side of the photograph. The road itself was only built in 1822, prior to that date, all the traffic through the town had to use the 'old' road which is behind the wall to the left-hand side, in front of the town's oldest church, the Parish Church of St. Lawrence. This old road, however, was itself superseded by Park Road, due to the steep hill in front of the church. To the right, centre, the tower of Chorley Town Hall is visible.

THE NORTH ENTRANCE, CHORLEY

L. Berry & Son

2 The steepness of the hill which formed a part of the old road through the town can be seen here. This was called Church Brow. It is not hard to realise why this road was superseded by Park Road, as on the previous photograph, for it must have caused many problems in the days of the stage coach, when the horses would have to work very hard to get up the steep hill. Dominating the hill is the Parish Church of St. Lawrence, which dates back to the 14th century. Before Park Road was built, the doorway on the left-hand side of the photograph was used by the town's residents who lived to the north of the church. Although having been unused for some 150 years, the doorway and adjoining walls have been preserved, and are within the St. Lawrence's Conservation Area today.

3 Another view of the Parish Church, this time looking from the south-west. In front of the church the steep Church Brow can be seen. At one time, at the bottom of this hill, the River Chor, which gives its name to the town, flowed across the road, most likely having had a place where the wagons and coaches would have to ford the stream. This stream is now culverted, and not visible here, although it is visible flowing through the parkland. The aisles, at each side of the stone tower, were built in 1861. The old 'turnpike road' can be seen in front of the church, descending to 'Chorley Bottoms', where the River Chor may well have had to be forded by the carriages. The churchyard gates are still the same today, but slightly angled across the corner. This was done during the 1960's when the old 'Church Brow' was filled in, to allow the main carriageway of Park Road to be widened.

Parish Church, Chorley

4 Before 1861. In the side aisles added to the nave of the church, the building fabric was very much the same as it had been for some 250 years or so, when the church was built, replacing the earlier 'chapel', which itself may have dated back to even earlier than the 14th century. By 1860 though, the church had become too small, and money was raised to add the aisles, which, according to some people at the time, meant that this additional building 'spoiled the look' of the old church. Today, in 1997, history repeats itself, for yet another addition is being put onto the church, and the same thing is being said by many today, that the new part will 'spoil' the old view; only time will tell.

5   In this view of Chorley Town Hall, the front of the building is decorated with flags and bunting, which is also draped across Market Street, a continuation of Park Road which we saw earlier. The decorations were in honour of the Coronation of King George V, which was in June of the year 1911. The rather plain looking building at the left of the picture was a public house called 'The Anchor'. Just beyond the Town Hall, also on the left, is another public house called 'The Red Lion'. On the site where the 'new' town hall was built there was another inn, which was, like the Red Lion, a coaching stop, for refreshments etc. This was the 'Gillibrand Arms'.

TOWN HALL, CHORLEY, SHEWING CORONATION DECORATIONS

A267/1012

6   In this view, from almost the same position as the previous picture, the narrow street in front of the Town Hall can be seen, in fact the street is narrow between the Old Town Hall on the right-hand side, and the 'new' one on the left. The Old Town Hall was built in 1802 following a donation of money to the town by a Mr. John Hollinshead. It was used as offices for the town guardians upstairs, having a butter market on the ground floor. This old building was demolished in the 1880's, but for a time, Chorley had two Town Halls. As the new town hall replaced the old one, some concern was raised about the sale of local dairy produce, which had been sold within the old town hall. In fact this same type of market was carried on in the basement of the new town hall.

7   One of the streets off Market Street led to the Market, where stalls, covered in the early days by canvas, served as a cover against the elements. But the stall covers were not too good, and would allow the rain to blow onto the stalls. This view is looking up the street towards the market stalls. The street is called Fazackerley Street, having shops at each side, and is one of the main shopping streets of the town today, as it was when this view was taken about 1920. Surprisingly, today's view up this street has changed little, as far as the street itself is concerned, although the market stalls have been much improved, along with the clearance of the buildings in the distance, to create a shopping mall in 1995.

FAZAKERLEY STREET, CHORLEY

8 Taken about the same date as the previous photograph, this view is taken from the opposite side of the market looking back towards Fazackerley Street which can be seen over the top of the market stalls. Surprisingly, the type of stall visible here, was still the same up to a few years ago only, when the market was upgraded, yet the stalls still retain their individuality and the market is essentially as it was years ago, but much drier. Near the covered market is a large open area which used to be a cattle market, used today as a visiting traders' market. This is nicknamed the 'Flat Iron'.

9   At the east end of the market runs a street by the name of New Market Street. This 1870's photograph shows some of the buildings in that street. These are: on the left, yet another public house called the 'Prince of Wales' and on the right, another one called the 'Fazackerley Arms'. Between the two pubs is one of the town's vetinary surgeons. The five carts in the street appear to be from the local brewery of the time at Whittle Springs, a short distance to the north of Chorley. As mentioned in a previous caption, these buildings have been cleared in 1994 and re-built in 1995. However, during demolition, it was possible to see former stables and haylofts behind the Fazackerly Arms, hidden from view until demolition.

10 Dated 9th August 1899, the persons on the photograph are ladies who were members of the St. Mary's Church Cycling Club, here seen getting ready for a ride out of the town. One of the favourite places to visit in those days were the springs mentioned below the previous photograph. These were mineral water springs, located close to the canal passing to the east of Chorley, and adjacent to the convergence of the Leeds to Liverpool Canal with the Lancaster Canal. Another view taken shortly after the lady cyclists have set off from the location shown in the photograph is rather interesting, in that it shows a reverend gentleman, who is also on a bicycle. This gives rise to the question 'was he acting as chaperone'?

11 This view shows one of the roads leading out of Chorley running to the west. Its name today is St. Thomas Road. Here we are looking back to the town centre and the Town Hall, the clock tower of which is visible above the roofs. To the right is Devonshire Road. The other building at the left side is the former police station, now re-built. Between the police station and the town hall is Town Hall Square. This site was the former 'town green' from the 16th century. It was on the 'town green' that markets and fairs would be held. Here was sited a large stone column, called 'the obelisk'. At this obelisk proclamations were made, whippings were car-ried out, and even wives were sold, at least two of these sales having been recorded. Our photograph dates from around the year 1900.

ST THOMAS'S ROAD, CHORLEY.

12   Moving south, past the town centre, where the town hall is located, we are in the main street passing through Chorley, and in the main shopping area of the town. The name is derived from the fact that cattle sales were conducted in this street during the 18th century. To the right-hand side, nearest, is the end of Chapel Street, and further on Fazackerley Street, then High Street. On the left, behind the railings, are the gardens and presbytery of St. Mary's Roman Catholic church. As to the actual date of the photograph we are uncertain, but we know it was pre-1910. The reason why is that in 1910 a stone archway was built at the far end of the railings. This arch was built to commemorate the 25 years that the incumbent of St. Mary's, Canon Crank, at the time had been in the priesthood.

CHORLEY. MARKET STREET.

13 Taken in the 1890's, this old photograph of Chorley's Market Street has many interesting facets to it. Just visible in the distance is the clock tower of the Town Hall. Along the cobbled street many horses and carts are engaged on their businesses. The nearest cart is owned by Messrs. 'Brindle and Son', who were furniture and carpet dealers, their shop being adjacent to the cart being loaded. On the left, nearest to the camera, is a pair of thatched cottages with shuttered windows. Across Market Street, on the right, we see the end of St. George's Street, on the nearest corner of which is Messrs. Booths Shop. This company was formed in 1847 in an adjacent town, the Chorley shop being the first one to be established away from the parent business location. The shop, after at least two rebuilds, is still in the same location today.

14 Taken from almost the same location as the previous photograph, we have 'moved on' some twenty years or so since then, to a date of around 1905. It would seem as if the 'age of the motor car' had not as yet arrived, at least there are none to be seen as yet. At the right-hand side nearest the camera is a street end. This is Halliwell Street, named after a local family. At the corner of this street is another shop which was popular at the time and in subsequent years, this was 'Rushtons'. Surprisingly, after ninety years or so, the shop fronts are still very much the same today, as they were when the photograph was taken, even traces of the painted signs on the shop walls are still visible.

MARKET STREET, CHORLEY

15 Another of the streets running away from Market Street is this, St. George's Street. This street with its church at the top end is a conservation area today. This is yet another of Chorley's streets which has changed very little since this old photograph was taken about the turn of the century. The church of St. George was built in 1825 at a cost of almost 14,000 pounds, half the cost of a modest house today. The church was one of those which was built out of a fund of one million pounds, allocated by the government for the building of new churches. The church has a gallery and can accommodate some two thousand persons.

ST. GEORGE'S CHURCH AND STREET, CHORLEY.   56780.J.V.

16 At the southern end of the main street through Chorley, Market Street, the road divides into two: the main road continuing towards Bolton and Manchester, and the other one running west, ultimately to Wigan, some nine miles away. This latter road is shown here, running out of town, in Pall Mall, towards Moor Road. On the left of the photograph is the St. George's Church Institute. The men of this institute were the builders of this temporary decorative arch crossing the road to the Eagle and Child public house on the right. The reason for the building of the archway was to celebrate the Coronation of King George V in 1911.

17   Another of the activities of the St. George's Mens Institute, when they were not building temporary arches that is, was playing bowls. In this part of England, bowls is played on 'crown greens', meaning that the bowling green itself is slightly raised in the centre of the grassed area. Flat greens are used in other areas of the country as well as crown greens. The church bowling club of St. George's had its own green, with a small pavilion, as can be seen on this view dating from about 1920. At today's modern church club bowling still provides much of the competitive atmosphere, some eighty years or so after the photograph was taken.

ST. GEORGES. BOWLING GREEN

18   Returning to the north end of Market Street, this splendid view, dating from the early 1900's, shows both of the Town Halls, the old and the new. The old one being on the right, with the advertisement for 'Yates, Saddler, Collar and Harness Maker' on the wall. On the left, the 'new' town hall of 1879. The event taking place is one of the local churches' 'Walks of Witness', locally called 'Walking Day'. Also visible is Park Road running to the left, and just to the right of the banner being carried, is the old main road running past the front of the parish church with a steep hill.

19   Another view of the town churches' 'Walking Day' event, is shown on this picture of about 1925. The location is the main street through the town, the procession passing the public house called the 'White Bull Inn'. The girls in the procession, and the banner being carried, are from St. Mary's Church. These 'Walking Day' processions are still held each year, when children and adults from their respective churches walk along the town's streets, and around their own parishes, to confirm their 'belonging' to that church. As 'witnessed' by those watching the event.

20 Thought to date from the 1890's, this view looks across the old 'cattle market' or 'Flat Iron' from Union Street. It shows a large gathering of people who seem to have either just taken part in some sort of religeous parade, or are about to start on one. The large building at the right-hand side of the photograph is a wooden one, destroyed by fire in 1914. This was a theatre called 'Sante's'.

An interesting point about this photograph is that there is, to the upper left of the centre, a very tall gas lamp, at least twice the height of an-other well-known Chorley gas lamp, nicknamed 'Big Lamp'. Do we have a 'bigger Big Lamp' here?

21 Chorley and district has a total of 23 separate townships or parishes around it, amounting to an area of over 82 square miles. Many of these townships, still 'in Chorley', have their own picturesque locations and churches. One of these is the village of Croston, the church here used to be the main church for the district, Chorley 'Chapel' coming under the control of Croston. To the right of the cross pedestal and pump in the foreground used to be a blacksmith's shop. In its latter days as a 'shop', it was used to assemble new bicycles, from parts purchased around the area. Thus the new bicycles were 'Made in Croston'.

CHURCH STREET, CROSTON

22 Croston Parish Church with its surrounding buildings has much for the visitor to look at. It is pleasing aesthetically… it has an interesting history… and it is architecturally pleasing to the eye. In this view, we are looking at the east end of the church from Church Meadows. On the left-hand side, the range of buildings here form a school dating from the 17th century and still in use today. Behind the school buildings, and off the photograph on the left-hand side, runs the River Yarrow, flowing through the village of Croston on its way to join the rivers Douglas and Ribble, thence to the sea some ten miles away.

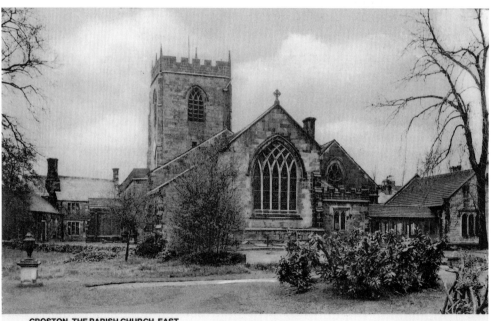

CROSTON, THE PARISH CHURCH, EAST

23 The old rectory adjacent to Croston Parish Church is one that has been photographed and painted on canvas many times. Its architecture is referred to as being of 'Dutch' style, looking at the photograph of the rectory being self-explanatory. This view dates from the 1930's and shows the front of the house, which has been here from about 1700. The building is currently having a new lease of life as a nursing home for the elderly, having been sold by the church into private hands. The whole area around the church, rectory, and street leading to the church, are designated as a conservation area.

CROSTON, THE RECTORY

24 North-east of Chorley lies another small village called Brindle. Here too is another old church dating back to the 17th century, which is located in the middle of this small community. Like so many of the villages in the Chorley rural area, agriculture is the main type of work being carried out, despite small amounts of other industries which have come and gone over the years. Brindle has been spared any industrial invasion, and remains today as it has been for generations, even its public house, 'The Cavendish Arms', being next-door to the church.

25 Rivington is a very scenic township lying to the south-east of Chorley. It is located at the edge of high country and the moorlands. It has been the site for the construction of large water reservoirs, which have created an area of out-standing beauty, amid the hills and valleys, often re-ferred to as a local 'lake dis-trict'. The whole of the area of Rivington is included in a protected zone, the immedi-ate area around the village being in Lever Park. This photograph shows the parish church in Rivington Village, which has its origins in the 15th century.

26 Staying in Rivington Village for this view, we see here the Nonconformist Chapel, located across the village green from the parish church. Like the churchyard opposite, there are many old datestones to be seen in the chapel graveyard, which have been brought from old farms etc. in the area, following their demolition. Buried in this chapel graveyard is Samuel Oldknow, a manufacturer of muslin, who was allegedly the first to produce this type of cloth in Lancashire in the 1790's. The chapel building still retains its box pews dating back to its building in 1703, and is one of the earliest in Lancashire. Adjoining the chapel on its east side, is a tiny house comprising one room upstairs and one downstairs. This was the former home of the minister at the chapel until 1787, when a manse was built a short distance away.

27   Still on the theme of churches in the Chorley district, this is the parish church of St. Mary in Eccleston, lying west of Chorley on the lowland part of the land hereabouts. This photograph dates from around 1905, and shows the front gateway entrance to the churchyard, which at this time was only a third of the size that it is today. This is another of the local churches which has featured on many a canvas, its natural red sandstone and pleasant setting being attractive to the painter. The River Yarrow runs along the lefthand side of the photograph, and forms the churchyard boundary. At times when in flood, the river has the churchyard completely covered with water.

28 I mentioned the lowland area to the west of Chorley in the previous caption. Here is an opposite, a view taken in the 1920's in Brinscall Village. This, like Rivington, is one set amidst hills with high moorlands on their top such as the hill shown in the distance. The event seems to be similar to the ones held in the town of Chorley, a church 'walking day', the banner being proudly held aloft, stating that it is from St. Luke's Church School. Despite its rural location, Brinscall had a small amount of industrial invasion. A Calico Printing Works was built here in the 19th century, and is now demolished. Stone quarrying is another old industry of the village, which still continues today.

29 This postcard is dated 1924 when it was sent from Chorley to Leicester. It shows three views of the town and district. The top illustration shows yet another view of Rivington with one of its lakes, to which we will come back later. The middle view shows the Roman Catholic church of Weldbank, Chorley. This was the firt Catholic church built in the town; before this, worship was done in one of the local halls of the gentry, in a private chapel. The bottom view shows the entrance into Chorley from the north. Just visible in the centre right of the lower photograph, the old entrance into Astley Park. At that time, there was an entrance lodge-house, the sole job of the occupant here was to ensure that only 'authorised persons' would come through the gates.

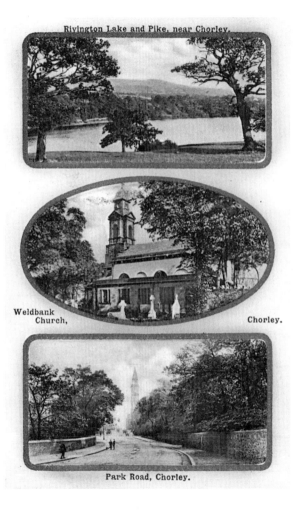

Rivington Lake and Pike, near Chorley.

Weldbank Church, Chorley.

Park Road, Chorley.

30 Chorley is very lucky in that it has a large number of grand houses, or used to have at least, but there are still many to see. There are other interesting public buildings as well, to be found in and around the town. One such building was this one shown on the photograph. It is the Public Library with its grand ornamentation. This building was donated to the town by Mr. Herbert Parke of Withnell Fold near Chorley and was opened in 1899. Before this date there had been a 'union library' established in 1814, and a 'Mechanics Institute' with reading room from 1844.

Public Library, Chorley

31 This building, located in the middle of the town, in Union Street, was built in 1906. It was the new 'Technical School', opened by the Earl of Derby. The school was soon to become the town's Grammar School, the third to hold this title. It continued to be Chorley Grammar School until the early 1960's, when a fourth school was built on the outskirts of the town. This became Parklands High School. The building in the photograph, however, had a new lease of life, becoming a teachers' training college. In 1986 the building was refurbished to be shared between Chorley Educational Offices and Chorley Central Library. The former library building in the previous photograph was demolished subsequently.

New Technical School, Chorley

32 Of the ancient halls of the former gentry of the town and district, Chorley is fortunate in having perhaps the best of these old buildings within the town itself, and situated in its own parkland. This is Astley Hall, the south front is shown in the view here. The hall was built in 1577 and was originally a timber construction. Over the centuries it has had many alterations, but remains today as it was when last lived in as a private dwelling in the early years of this century. The building is a big attraction with visitors to the town, and houses the town's Art Gallery and a large amount of period furniture. The plasterwork ceilings are also of great interest.

ASTLEY HALL, CHORLEY.

33 The entrance hall to Astley Hall itself is shown here as it was in the early 1900's, and would be as it was when last occupied. Note the small portion of the splendid leather and lead sculptured ceiling of the hall, which is visible at the top of the photograph. The hall has belonged to the families of Charnock, Brooke and Towneley Parker over the centuries, and was presented to the town as a war memorial by R.A. Tatton after the First World War. The staircase on the left side is one which causes some discussion, for as one goes up the steps to the first floor, the height of each step decreases. In view of the age of this staircase, this inno-vation, designed for ease of climbing stairs, could certain-ly be incorporated into modern staircases.

34 To the 'back' of Astley Hall is a small, almost self-contained 'mini hall' which is attached to the main building. Although this part of the building is 'out of sight', it is nevertheless a portion of the hall which raises questions as to its association with the main building, for this rather attractive small building may well have had its origins before the main hall was built. At the other side of this building is a walled garden. This would provide the vegetables and fruit which would grace the table of the main hall. Although greater interest is now being expressed in the restoration of gardens of this type nationally, Astley Hall's former Kitchen Garden still awaits rejuvenation.

35 Astley Park formed a part of the town's war memorial, and a cenotaph to the memory of the Chorley men who died during the First World War was built just inside the front entrance to the park. The official opening of the park with its cenotaph was in 1924. This undated postcard is believed to date from the first year of the cenotaph's dedication, in 1924, hence the huge crowd of people in attendance. The cenotaph itself was designed on the lines of the old 'town obelisk', which stood on Town Green behind the Town Hall. The town obelisk was a tall shaft of stone with a cross on its top. It was used as a meeting and/or selling place, and even a place of punishment; whippings are recorded to have taken place here, and even wives were sold as well? As part of the Millenium Celebrations, it has been mooted that the old town obelisk be re-erected.

THE "CENOTAPH" CHORLEY.   400.

ALLEN & SONS.
OLDHAM & BLACKPOOL.

36 This is a view looking down the main driveway of Astley Park just past the cenotaph, which is on the left-hand side. On the extreme right, in the valley, the River Chor flows through this parkland. If one continues to walk along this main driveway, Astley Hall itself is reached about three quarters of a mile further on. Or one can walk through the mature woodland to the centre left, to reach the hall with its associated duckpond. Large open areas of parkland before arriving at the hall have been laid out for sporting activities, and beyond the hall are bowling greens and tennis courts.

ASTLEY PARK, CHORLEY.

37 Still in Chorley's Astley Park, and a little way down the main driveway, prior to entering the mature woodlands, we arrive at this 'paddling pool'. This pool used to be a focal point for young children and their families, until recent times when 'health and safety' problems seem to have come to light. Many Chorley people will, I know, recall happy times spent at this location, including myself. But the future of the pool is uncertain, and it might well soon become just a memory. The water running into the pool came from a natural spring in an adjacent field, the original Chorley Golf Course. It was here that my own younger days were spent, near the spring, which over all the years remained a constant flow and its water was always cold and refreshing to drink.

COPYRIGHT CHILDREN'S PADDLING POOL AND ASTLEY PARK, CHORLEY LILYWHITE LT BRIGHOUSE

38 Another of Chorley's halls was this one, unfortunately demolished in the early 1950's, like so many other have been in the area. This was called Duxbury Hall and, like Astley, had its own parkland surrounding it. The hall was rather plain in design, and was to occupy this site, it had only been built in the 18th century, although the ancient family associated with this hall, the 'Duxbury's', were living in the area in the 13th century. In later times, the hall came into the ownership of the Standish family, of which a famous 'son' was Miles Standish, of the Pilgrim Fathers period. It has been speculated for a long time that Miles was born at Duxbury, but there is no conclusive proof of this.

39　Gillibrand Hall is of similar design to that of Duxbury, and is still in use today as a home for the elderly. Another name that this hall used to have was Lower Chorley Hall; this was in the 17th and 18th century, prior to the building of the present hall. Close by the hall was Home Farm, where a stone barn was located which had accommodation for the groom and coachmen of the hall. That barn is shown here in rather delapidated condition, but it has since been restored and is now a private residence. It would seem that horses were not just on the ground floor in this building, there was evidence that they were taken up the steps to the first floor as well.

40 This photograph shows the front of Euxton (pronounced Exton) Hall, another 18th-century hall built on the site of successive earlier halls. It was the home of the Anderton family. In the 1920's the hall upper floor was removed, to leave a 'bungalow' style hall, which survives today and is now a private hospital. Although regarded as being of 'plain' architectural style, it was nevertheless an imposing building prior to its reduction in height. All the people posing on the picture seem to be staff or employees. In the left foreground perhaps the gamekeeper complete with gun and dog. In the doorway of the house servants, and in front of the house gardeners.

41   Although much smaller in size when compared with, say, the previous Euxton Hall, this building is also in the township of Euxton, and is vaguely connected with Euxton Hall. This other hall, shown on the photograph here, is called Buckshaw Hall, and was the home of the Robinson family. It was built in the 1660's on land given to the Robinson family by the Andertons of Euxton Hall. This old hall, although in poor condition today, will be fully restored in the not too distant future. This photograph dates from about 1880. The photograph can be roughly dated from the fact that, in 1882, the roof was stripped of its flagstones and a slate roof was fitted. At the same time the timber gables were altered to a different style to what they are today.

42 To the west of Chorley is the township of Charnock Richard. Here, at Park Hall, was the seat of the Darlington family, who were great benefactors to the local community. The hall, which has been mentioned for some seven hundred years at this site, has had many rebuilds. Today the hall has been made into a hotel and nightclub, and is the location of the leisure complex called 'Camelot'. During the 1970's, part of the leisure complex site was a horse jumping arena, called 'Arena North'. It was here that the film 'International Velvet' was partially made. Just off the photograph on the right-hand side is a large pond. Although this served as an ornamental feature adjacent to the hall, it was in fact a mill pond, holding a reserve of water to drive a water corn mill a short way downstream.

PARK HALL CHARNOCK RICHARD nr CHORLEY

43 The name of Ellerbeck is locally associated with a stream of that name which flows through the area where yet another local hall stood until a few years ago. This was the home of the Hodson family from the late 18th century. Through marriage the Ellerbeck Estate, which was in Duxbury, became the seat of the Cardwells. This family were much engaged in politics. Perhaps the best known member of the family was Edward Cardwell, who had a distinguished career in government, beginning in 1842, under Mr. Gladstone. He was Chancellor of the Duchy of Lancaster and Secretary for War. He became Viscount Cardwell in 1874. The photograph dates from the turn of the century, circa 1900. Because of opencast coal mining operations nearby, the hall was demolished in the mid-1970's.

44   We have seen illustrations of the church and chapel at Rivington Village, to the south-east of Chorley. Here now is Rivington Hall, once the home of the squires of Rivington. The hall, the origins of wich date back to the 15th century, has had several alterations/extensions put onto it, its front now being of 'Georgian' style. This view shows the entrance gates into the hall gardens taken about 1900. Evidence of the hall's earlier years, when it was the home of the local squire, can be found at the back of the main building, in the U-shaped courtyard, where the walls are of blackened stone, which incorporate datestones of 1712 along with initials of the Breres, then the squires of Rivington. The present hall was built in 1780.

RIVINGTON HALL.

5

45   Adjoining the hall is the Hall Barn. This used to form part of the agricultural side of the squires estate, and was being used for hay storage and/or animal accommodation. The hall and estates were sold by a Mr. Crompton in 1898, and bought by Mr. W.H. Lever, a soap manufacturer from Bolton, whose business was established at Port Sunlight near Birkenhead. A great amount of alteration and improvement work was carried out in the immediate area to create ornamental gardens on a steep hillside, to build follies, and to build himself a new dwelling. This photograph shows Rivington Hall Barn, converted for use as a concert/dance/tea venue in 1911.

INTERIOR. RIVINGTON HALL BARN

46 Another local 'hall' type building, yet described as a 'house', is this one at Bretherton, to the west of Chorley. It is called Carr House. Its greatest claim to fame is its association with the astronomer Jeremiah Horrocks, who was a member of the clergy at the nearby parish church in Hoole. The house itself has a datestone which states that it was built in 1613. It was, however, 1639 when Jeremiah Horrocks proved his calculations whilst at Carr House and observed the first transit of the planet Venus across the face of the sun. The house had a period when it accommodated a large collection of dolls, which are now exhibited at Lancaster. Today the house is in private ownership once again.

47   Between Chorley and Bretherton, the most westerly part of Chorley's outlying parishes, lies Euxton; we have already seen two of the halls which lie in this parish. Here is a third hall. This is called Runshaw Hall, and was the home of a local industrialist from its building in the 19th century. Since its vacation as a private house, it has been used by the Brothers of Charity, and as a restaurant. It is now undergoing refurbishment after a fire, the hall being converted once more into residential accommodation. The photograph shows the hall when used as a private house and is dated to about 1920.

48   A few photographs back, I mentioned some of the attractions of Rivington village and parish. This time I will say little, but let the photographs prove the point… firstly a view which shows one of the water reservoirs with the hillside and moorlands behind. The hill, with the small tower on top of it, is called Rivington Pike and is a popular viewpoint. From the top of this hill one looks west to the Irish Sea some 25 miles away, the Isle of Man also being visible on a clear day. Below the summit of the hill can be seen an area of trees, apparently forming a corner. These trees and shrubs, now much overgrown, are within the former garden created by Lord Lever, more photographs of these will follow.

Pike and Lake   Rivington

49 That small 'eminence' visible on the top of the hill in the previous photograph is shown here in close up. It is a small tower that was built in 1733. As to whether or not its function was purely decorative is uncertain, but it was used in the days of grouse shooting on the adjoining moors by the squire's shooting parties. Inside a fire was built and food was provided for the shooting parties. This hill, on which the tower is built, was known during the 16th to 18th centuries as Riven Pike. It formed the site of one of the chain of fire beacons throughout the land, which warned of the coming of the Spanish Armada in 1588.

50 Following his purchase of the Rivington estates etc. Mr. Lever built himself a bungalow at the hillside overlooking Rivington. Around the bungalow, and on the steep hillside, which was formerly rough ground, he had built the most wonderful gardens. Some of their features being cascades and waterfalls, grottoes, exotic species of plants and trees, a Japanese garden, bridges and decorative entrance lodges. All this work cost in the region of £131,000 between his purchase of the estate and 1905. Our photograph shows the first bungalow, a wooden one, which was set on fire by the suffragette movement in July 1913.

THE BUNGALOW, RIVINGTON.

Nº3.

51 Not to be deterred from his intention of living at Rivington following the destruction of the wooden bungalow, the site was soon cleared of debris, and a new bungalow built. This time it was built of stone and concrete, the cost being some £30,000. In this view of the stone bungalow we can also see, on the right-hand side, a short stone column. This is the cross shaft which forms the lower part of the 'Headless Cross' in Anderton Village. At the time when the photograph was taken, about 1920, Lord Lever, as he had now become, had many of the old datestones and other 'curios' of any age brought to the bungalow gardens, for 'safe keeping'. The estate was put up for sale again in 1947, being purchased by Liverpool Corporation Water Works, and most of the buildings were demolished.

THE BUNGALOW, RIVINGTON

52   One of the gatehouses into the bungalow grounds of Lord Lever at Rivington is shown in this view. The gate lodges into the gardens were at their busiest when, at certain times in the year, the private gardens would be open to the general public. The first such occasion was in 1919, when, for a small fee, the money being given to local charities etc., the public were first allowed to view this 'Panorama of Beauty', as the papers stated. The flowering trees and plants were out in profusion, and the general public in their thousands strolled the grounds at their leisure, to see the waterfalls, lawns, flowers, dove cote, pergolas, terraces and balconies. It was estimated that a total of over 4,000 persons were in attendance on this first opening day. Local charity organisations were presented with almost £80 received from the attendees on the first open day of the gardens. And of the zoo as well, of course.

LEVERS PARK, RIVINGTON.

53 Yet another of the magnificent works of Lord Lever in Rivington was the building of this great folly. It is a reconstruction of the ruinous Liverpool Castle, as it was recorded during that castle's latter days in Liverpool during the 17th century. It is full size, and accessible to the general public. It stands on the west side of one of the reservoirs built at Rivington by Liverpool Corporation, during the 1850's, to supply drinking water to Liverpool, some 20 miles away. Standing as it does on slightly raised ground, it is hardly possible to realise that this is actually a folly, created in Lever Park, and not 'genuine'. It is certainly a surprise 'find' to the first-time visitor here.

54 Located south of Chorley is the township of Anderton, its name was also that of the lords of this manor, who lived at the manorial hall. One of the farms near Anderton Hall is called 'Roscoe Lowe'. It was the home of the Foster family, who were tenants of the Andertons. A daughter of this family married Samuel Oldknow, who came from Nottingham. They lived here at Roscoe Lowe Farm and, with a Joseph Shaw, set up a textile business. Samuel died at the age of 25 years in 1759, but the business was continued by his widow and partner. This partnership was a very successful one, and they employed many domestic weavers in the district. In 1764, the first British muslin cloth was manufactured at Roscoe Lowe Farm, in a workshop which had been created in the upper floor of the building on the right in the photograph. Samuel was buried in the chapel in nearby Rivington Village.

55 Many of the early industries in the Chorley area used water power as a driving medium. There are known sites of perhaps a dozen or so of this type of mill scattered along the rivers around the town. The earliest of this type was used to grind corn and later fulling mills and cotton mills were built on the streams. Our photograph shows the location of two water-driven mills, although the photograph dates from the early 1900's, and the mill in the centre of the picture is now steam-driven, the water wheel having been removed. The water coming out of the sluice at the lower left of the picture is from the mill race which powered a corn mill, that used to stand off the photograph, on the left. The mills described here got their power from the River Yarrow. The location of the mills was at Armetryding in Euxton.

56 By the end of the 19th century, the production of cotton goods had become the biggest employer in the Chorley district. Large three- and four-storey mills had appeared, and were built with great architectural flair, their exteriors being decorated with terra cotta of various colours. Four such mills were built in the Chorley area between about 1906 and 1912. These four mills were all built by the same company, all had the same type of driving engines, and they all had similar decoration on their external walling. They were built at the zenith of mill construction, and incorporated all the latest technology and design. Two of these mills are shown here in the early 1900's, they were both in the township of Coppull, and were called Mavis Mill and Coppull Ring Mill.

57 Another of these four mills is shown in this photograph. This is Talbot Mill, or Bagganley Mill, in Chorley, built alongside the canal. This mill was the biggest in the county of Lancashire when built, having the unique situation of being two mills in one. The two mills can be seen in the photograph. On the left, the four-storey part of the building was used for the process of spinning, and on the right, the single-storey part was the weaving 'shed'. Between the two mills can be seen the driving engine house. This had two seperate engines, one to drive the spinning mill and the other to drive the weaving shed. The spinning section of this grand mill was demolished during 1995, the weaving section is still at work. The mill was built alongside the Leeds to Liverpool Canal, and canal transport used to bring raw cotton to the mill as well as coal for the boilers. The official name of the mill, Talbot, stems from the historical association with the mill's location.

58 The Leeds to Liverpool Canal, running on the east side of Chorley, has provided a corridor of transport for canal boats since it was opened in 1797. Then it was the Lancaster Canal, the Leeds to Liverpool Company's 'cut' joined the Lancaster at Whittle Springs to the north of Chorley in 1816. The canal was used for the conveyance of goods until the 1950's, declining to give way to road transportation. In the photograph, barges are seen approaching the Chorley section of the canal. At the front, nearest to the camera, is a boat with engine, a 'flyboat' or 'tug'. This is pulling the other four barges, which have no engines, but are loaded almost down to water level.

59 The canal was not solely used for the transportation of goods, however. The boats, prior to having engines fitted into them, were pulled by horses. The speed of the horse-drawn barges was quite slow and leisurely. This was perhaps the reason for their popularity, as a means of providing outings for groups of people, in large numbers. Churches, Sunday schools etc. frequently used one of the empty barges to transport them a few miles away from Chorley, to some suitable location for their picnic, eventually returning home the same way. Having experienced some of these outings, I recall the enjoyment of them, and how it was possible to see so much wildlife, due to the absence of an engine to drive the barge. This photograph dates from about 1910.

60 Another of the rural villages of Chorley is Eccleston, some four miles out of the town to the west. Like most of the other villages around Chorley, it has an interesting history, many of the old places still being visible, such as the parish church, the water mill and two moated sites. Traces of much earlier occupation in the form of worked flint has been found here, as it has further west in Croston. Our photograph, although 'old', is certainly not thousands of years old, but only about one hundred. It shows Dole Cottage in Eccleston, which was the home of the Bretherton family. A cobbler's workshop was located in the cottage which was run by the Bretherton family. In the photograph Mr. Bretherton, his son and employee Mr. Threlfall, all wearing aprons, are in the company of a visitor. He was Mr. Edward Wane, with walking stick.

61   In Chorley we have seen photographs of the Town Hall and referred to its opening in 1879. This photograph was taken at the same date as those, in 1879. For the grand opening of the new building, many events were organized to celebrate the occasion. One of the events was a procession of floats, illustrating Chorley's modern approach to its industries etc. In addition to the industrial floats, the Corporation itself had floats, to show the public what was being done or planned for the town in the future. One of these floats is seen here. This one shows how coal gas was produced, for gas was being installed in the households of the town at this time. The first gas to light a Chorley Street was used in 1819. This was 'surplus to requirements' of the adjacent cotton spinning mill of Timothy Lightoller in Standish Street.

62   In Chorley in 1892, this spontaneous looking photograph was taken outside the cottages that stood on the main road going out of the town to the north, Preston Road. It was close to this location, that the Toll Gate was placed across the road to prevent vehicles entering the town at night, during the 18th century. The cottages themselves – which have now been long demolished – were built during the early 1800's, and were built of stone. Today the Comet Store is at this location. In the 1890's, there were six fishmongers in Chorley, one at least of these having a delivery round as shown here. An additional point about the photograph is that it clearly shows the type of clothing worn in 1892.

63 This interesting old photograph shows Chorley in the late 19th century; it is thought to be a trade procession, although no advertising is visible on the carts. The view is looking south, along New Market Street, with Chapel Street in the distance. The buildings on the right-hand side are at the end of High Street. The large building on the left-hand side is one we have briefly mentioned before, the 'Grand Theatre' of Mr. Testo Sante, usually referred to as 'Santes'. The all wooden building was burned down in 1914, which was a great loss to the general public of the town. Notice also some of the other interesting activities which are in the photograph, such as the ice cream sellers and the amusements at the left-hand side. Whatever the event, it looks like it was, as they say in Lancashire, a 'reet good do'.

64 Yet another of the townships or parishes of Chorley, is one called Heapey. This lies on the edge of the 'hill country' to the north-east of the town. Within the scattered township, which contains a large number of farms, are hamlets, comprising groups of cottages. One of these hamlets is called White Coppice, at the very edge of the moorland that rises abruptly from a water conduit, called the 'goit', which allows drinking water to flow between catchment reservoirs. This isolated community was born out of stone quarrying and lead mining. The picturesque hamlet has a cricket field which, from a natural beauty point of view, cannot be bettered, having a backdrop of high moorland hills and storage water lodges for the former works. The area is a local beauty spot and a popular picnic site. Our photograph shows the road approaching the cricket field, 'about 1880'. On the right is Warth Farm, and on the left, just visible, is Warth Brook itself.

65 Another 'hill country' village is Wheelton, near Chorley. This is divided into 'Higher' and 'Lower' areas according to their geographical position. This is another area which comprises many groupings or communities of houses etc. of a 'scattered' nature. Through Lower Wheelton runs the Leeds to Liverpool Canal, which drops down several locks, to emerge at Whittle Springs Basin where the Lancaster Canal ran northwards. Our photograph was taken in Lower Wheelton. It shows Messrs. Cowburn's butcher's shop. The shop can be seen with a counter accessed from the street. In the donkey cart are Herbert Cowburn, the son of the butcher at the time, plus a friend. The photograph was taken about 1916.

66 The village of Euxton, although rural, had several mills producing flour, paper, cotton goods, the earlier mills being powered by the River Yarrow which flows through the township in a westerly direction. One such mill was the water corn mill situated in the hamlet of Pincock, adjoining the river, at the southern end of Euxton. The photograph was taken outside this mill about 1900, and shows some of the men who worked for Mr. Ashworth, the owner of the mill at the time, together with horses and wagons. This site today is almost totally overgrown and clear of any permanent structures. Today the mill leat is still visible with traces of the tail race from the mill back to the river Yarrow.

67 This view of Pincock Hamlet was taken from the main road passing through the village and looking westwards. The view looks over the roof of the mill we have seen in the previous photograph. The water mill itself was in the building to the lower right of the photograph. Passing from left to right in the middle, the old 'turnpike road' can be seen, used until the 'new' road was built. Directly ahead can be seen Pincock Street, a community itself, a single street with terraced houses each side. At the back of the houses on the left is the River Yarrow. Also just visible in the distance are two mill chimneys. The left-hand one is at the 'Bobbin Shop' as it later became, at Armetryding, and the other, on the right, is at the cotton factory of Euxton Mill. Today the old hamlet has disappeared, but a row of new bungalows has been built to the right of the old street.

68 In the rural areas of Chorley, the encroaching motor vehicle got off to a 'slow start', the horse and cart were still largely in use during the post-war years and into the 1920's. Scenes like the one here were becoming less common. In the photograph, newly woven baskets are being taken from Maw-desley, a village to the south-west of Chorley, where basket making was carried out, to the railway station at Rufford. From here they were taken by train to many of the markets in Lancashire. To make the baskets, willows were grown in large amounts locally, and when of the required length, were 'harvested'. After pro-cessing, such as the removal of the bark, the 'twigs' as they were called, were allowed to dry partially. They were then used to make all manner of baskets, from those used for shopping, to large hampers etc.

69 An idea as to what Chorley looked like in the 1920's, can be gleaned from this photograph. It is one of the earliest aerial views of the town, taken about 1920. To anyone having a knowledge of the town's development since the photograph was taken, the difference today is hard to believe. The easiest way to describe the many aspects of the 1920's town in the photograph, is to use the railway to sort east from west. On the right, the east, numerous cotton mills with many open spaces, as yet to be built upon. In the left, centre, can be seen the large open area called the 'Flat Iron', where today's markets are held. At this time there were two gasometers, where the later Public Baths would be built in the 1930's.

70 The first bus service to run out of Chorley was started by the Lancashire and Yorkshire Railway Company in circa 1900, the date of this photograph. The buses were run from the railway station at Chorley northwards to the township of Bamber Bridge, a distance of about six miles from Chorley. Here, another of the routes of the L and Y Railway, one from Blackburn to Preston, crossed the main road. Here the station was built. It was between the stations of Chorley and Bamber Bridge that the bus route served, travelling through the intervening villages of Whittle le Woods and Clayton le Woods, taking passengers to and from the railway stations.

71   By the 1920's, travel by motor coach was the most popular way of having a day out, for Chorley and its villages are less than twenty miles from Southport, and thirty from Blackpool. Local bus services between the main towns were set up during the 1920's, but at weekends, it was the 'coach' or, as it was called, the charabanc, pronounced 'shara-bang'. These usually had a soft top which would be down if the weather was suitable. But I should think that they would be very draughty. In this photograph a party comprising of mostly ladies looks as if they are about to embark on their charabanc for a trip, probably to the seaside. The party is departing from the Alison Arms in Coppull. By the look of the vehicle with its hard tyres and style, it looks as if it is a 'war surplus'. It has the name 'Kitchener' on the side of the bonnet as well, suggesting a date of perhaps just pre-1920's.

72 Charabanc companies were extant from about 1910 in many local townships. The types of vehicle used varied, depending on the assets held by the owners. The places travelled to by the coaches on their day trips were usually the coastal resorts of Southport, Blackpool, Morecambe and Windermere in the main. Many other locations were on their itineraries also, some of them being inland, parks and favourite woodland picnic places. In Chorley the monopoly for day trips was held by the 'Parsons Motor Charabanc Company'. They had their offices in West Street, in the middle of Chorley, quite coincidentally near to the 'Yates' Wine Lodge', where, no doubt, 'one for the road' was often the order of starting, for it was outside this venue that the coaches started on their trips. Our photograph shows an outing about to set off, probably in the early 1920's. The coach itself would certainly be a collectors' item today.

73 The coming of the bus service to Chorley began at the turn of the century, although this was over a limited route only. Gradually more independent companies were formed, each covering their own particular routes to and from local towns and villages. Many of the buses were made locally by Leyland Motors. One of these can be seen in our photograph, showing a bus coming through Fazackerley Street in the mid-1920's. The other vehicles shown are also of interest, as are the shops, which will be recalled by older readers perhaps. Those with names such as 'Dunderdales', 'Illingworths' and the 'Chorley Co-operative Society' shop on the left. The street has not changed too much today, so far as its buildings are concerned, now forming part of a pedestrian precinct.

Market Place and Fazakerley St, Chorley.

"Empire View" 01091

74 Market Street in Chorley in the early 1930's. Cars have now replaced the horse and cart, here in the town at least. In this view we are looking to the north, with St. George's Street on the right-hand side. Again some of the shops are those which will be recalled by many, with names such as 'Royles' at one corner of St. George's Street, with 'Booths' at the other corner. The road surface of the street is cobbled, and would stay like this until after the Second World War, as would the other streets in the town. Notice too the minimal number of gas lamps for street lighting… here too, electricity was late in coming to the main street, in the early 1950's in fact.

MARKET STREET, CHORLEY.   G.9144

75 Another 1930's photograph catches a little bit of 'old Chorley'. Although not a special picture, it just shows someone getting on with day to day activities, which just happened to be recorded at the time... for posterity. The location is Bolton Road, which forms part of the main A6 road through the town, on the south side. Like Market Street, the road surface is cobbled. Across the other side of the road are stone-built cottages. These, and many like them, were located within the town, especially in Bolton Road, and the streets off this, such as Queen Street and King Street. All these cottages had cellars, which were used for the purpose of hand loom weaving from the early 19th century. Most of these cottages were demolished during the 1950's, although a few have been preserved and restored. In the foreground is Mr. Harrison, the proprietor of a shop here.

76   Although the infrastructure was now in place by the 1930's for the people of Chorley to travel to the seaside by charabanc as well as by train, not everyone could afford to do this. Fortunately, the town is situated on the edge of the high moorland to the east, whilst bordering in the west to level lowland countryside, thus providing a wide variety of scenic walks etc. The 1850's saw the building of Liverpool Corporations water storage reservoirs at Rivington, and since that time, the growth of trees around them has created a place of great scenic beauty on Chorleys 'doorstep'. Rivington, often described as a 'mini lakeland', is still as popular with visitors today as it has been since the 1920's. The illustration here is from a painting of the 'Rivington Lakes', painted by Frederick William Hulme, who lived between 1816 and 1884.